WHO IS JESUS?

IN HIS OWN WORDS

12 Studies for Individuals or Groups

RUTH E. VAN REKEN

SHAW

WATERBROOK
PRESS

Dedicated to my good friend, Barb Knuckles. "As iron sharpens iron, so one man sharpens another" (Proverbs 27:17). Thanks for being God's iron in my life—especially for this study. I love and appreciate you.

A special thanks also to my critique group members, who helped me with the fine tuning of words. And to Ann Kroeker and Mary Ellen Rothrock for their most helpful editorial skills!

WHO IS JESUS?
PUBLISHED BY WATERBROOK PRESS
12265 Oracle Boulevard, Suite 200
Colorado Springs, CO 80921

Unless otherwise indicated, all Scripture quotations are taken from the *Holy Bible: New International Version* ® *NIV* ® Copyright 1973, 1978, 1984 by International Bible Society. Used by permission of Zondervan Publishing House. All rights reserved.

ISBN: 978-0-87788-914-4

Published in the United States by WaterBrook Multnomah, an imprint of The Doubleday Publishing Group, a division of Random House Inc., New York

WATERBROOK and its deer colophon are registered trademarks of Random House Inc.

Cover photo © 1993 by Robert Moseley

Printed in the United States of America

CONTENTS

INTRODUCTION

In his book *Kingdoms in Conflict,* Charles Colson writes, "The shock waves that threaten the very foundations of our culture today . . . emanate from society's failure to understand man's need for God and the Christians' failure to accurately present Christ's message of the kingdom of God."

As Christians, we often try to define the kingdom of God by a set of rules and "how-tos." Yet we can't know the kingdom unless we know the king. By understanding the character of the king, we will then also know the character of his kingdom.

But how can we know this king? Our finite minds are far too limited to ever grasp the scope of who he is.

This is why Jesus came—to show us the Father. He says that he and the Father are one; if we know him we will also know the Father. Only because God has taken the initiative to reveal himself to us through Jesus Christ do we have any hope of knowing who he is or what his kingdom is.

When he stood before God at the burning bush, Moses asked who he should say had sent him to Egypt. God's reply was, "I AM WHO I AM. This is what you are to say to the Israelites: 'I AM has sent me to you.'" Thereafter, the children of Israel considered I AM to be one of God's holiest names.

Now Jesus makes a claim to that name. To the Pharisees who are upset with him, he says, "Before Abraham was born, I am." Each time he makes an "I am" statement, they know he is also claiming to be God. But in each "I am," Jesus further reveals who God is. He shows why Jesus is the only way for us to know God.

Whether this is your first Bible study or your hundredth, you will enjoy seeing more of who God is as Jesus' revelation unfolds in pictures we can understand.

HOW TO USE THIS STUDYGUIDE

Fisherman studyguides are based on the inductive approach to Bible study. Inductive study is discovery study; we discover what the Bible says as we ask questions about its content and search for answers. This is quite different from the process in which a teacher *tells* a group *about* the Bible and what it means and what to do about it. In inductive study God speaks directly to each of us through his Word.

A group functions best when a leader keeps the discussion on target, but this leader is neither the teacher nor the "answer person." A leader's responsibility is to *ask*—not *tell*. The answers come from the text itself as group members examine, discuss, and think together about the passage.

There are four kinds of questions in each study. The first is an *approach question*. Used before the Bible passage is read, this question breaks the ice and helps you focus on the topic of the Bible study. It begins to reveal where thoughts and feelings need to be transformed by Scripture.

Some of the earlier questions in each study are *observation questions* designed to help you find out basic facts—who, what, where, when, and how.

When you know what the Bible says you need to ask, *What does it mean?* These *interpretation questions* help you to discover the writer's basic message.

Application questions ask, *What does it mean to me?* They challenge you to live out the Scripture's life-transforming message.

Fisherman studyguides provide spaces between questions for jotting down responses and related questions you would like to raise in the group. Each group member should have a copy of the studyguide and may take a turn in leading the group.

For consistency, Fisherman guides are written from the *New International Version*. But a group should feel free to use the NIV or any other accurate, modern translation of the Bible such as the *New Living Translation*, the *New Revised Standard Version*, the *New Jerusalem Bible*, or the *Good News Bible*. (Other paraphrases of the Bible may be referred to when additional help is needed.) Bible commentaries should not be brought to a Bible study because they tend to dampen discussion and keep people from thinking for themselves.

SUGGESTIONS FOR GROUP LEADERS

1. Read and study the Bible passage thoroughly beforehand, grasping its themes and applying its teachings for yourself. Pray that the Holy Spirit will "guide you into truth" so that your leadership will guide others.

2. If the studyguide's questions ever seem ambiguous or unnatural to you, rephrase them, feeling free to add others that seem necessary to bring out the meaning of a verse.

3. Begin (and end) the study promptly. Start by asking someone to pray for God's help. Remember, the Holy Spirit is the teacher, not you!

4. Ask for volunteers to read the passages out loud.

5. As you ask the studyguide's questions in sequence, encourage everyone to participate in the discussion. If some are silent, ask, "What do you think, Heather?" or, "Dan, what can you add to that answer?" or suggest, "Let's have an answer from someone who hasn't spoken up yet."

6. If a question comes up that you can't answer, don't be afraid to admit that you're baffled! Assign the topic as a research project for someone to report on next week.

7. Keep the discussion moving and focused. Though tangents will inevitably be introduced, you can bring the discussion back to the topic at hand. Learn to pace the discussion so that you finish a study each session you meet.

8. Don't be afraid of silences: some questions take time to answer and some people need time to gather courage to speak. If silence persists, rephrase your question, but resist the temptation to answer it yourself.

9. If someone comes up with an answer that is clearly illogical or unbiblical, ask him or her for further clarification: "What verse suggests that to you?"

10. Discourage Bible-hopping and overuse of cross-references. Learn all you can from *this* passage, along with a few important references suggested in the studyguide.

11. Some questions are marked with a ♦. This indicates that further information is available in the Leader's Notes at the back of the guide.

12. For further information on getting a new Bible study group started and keeping it functioning effectively, read Gladys Hunt's *You Can Start a Bible Study Group* and *Pilgrims in Progress: Growing through Groups* by Jim and Carol Plueddemann.

SUGGESTIONS FOR GROUP MEMBERS

1. Learn and apply the following ground rules for effective Bible study. (If new members join the group later, review these guidelines with the whole group.)

2. Remember that your goal is to learn all that you can *from the Bible passage being studied.* Let it speak for itself without using Bible commentaries or other Bible passages. There is more than enough in each assigned passage to keep your group productively occupied for one session. Sticking to the passage saves the group from insecurity and confusion.

3. Avoid the temptation to bring up those fascinating tangents that don't really grow out of the passage you are discussing. If the topic is of common interest, you can bring it up later in informal conversation following the study. Meanwhile, help each other stick to the subject!

4. Encourage each other to participate. People remember best what they discover and verbalize for themselves. Some people are naturally shyer than others, or they may be afraid of making a mistake. If your discussion is free and friendly and you show real interest in what other group members think and feel, they will be more likely to speak up. Remember, the more people involved in a discussion, the richer it will be.

5. Guard yourself from answering too many questions or talking too much. Give others a chance to express themselves. If you are one who participates easily, discipline yourself by counting to ten before you open your mouth!

6. Make personal, honest applications and commit yourself to letting God's Word change you.

"I AM THE WAY"

John 13:33–14:14

When I was a child, my family lived overseas and we often traveled. Sometimes we went by propeller planes or on big, wonderful ocean liners like the SS *United States*. Other times we drove in a tiny, black 1946 Fordson, or rode on a sooty, coal-driven train. Each type of travel had its own peculiar sense of adventure, but there was one reason I dared to take them all. I was going with my father.

One night our car became stuck in a shallow river. We climbed out through the windows to spend the night on the riverbank. By morning, the car was completely submerged. I certainly had no idea how we would ever get to our vacation place, but as I held my father's hand while we walked to a nearby village looking for help, I knew one thing. My dad would get us where we were trying to go. I didn't need to know how, I just knew he could figure it all out. If I simply stayed with him, he would be my way to get there.

1. When you plan a trip, how do you prepare for the journey?

Read John 13:33–14:14.

2. Why is Jesus telling the disciples not to be troubled (14:1)? What is upsetting them?

3. Where does Jesus say he is going in 14:2-4? What do you think he means?

4. What promises does Jesus make to his disciples (14:3)?

5. Which of Jesus' statements does Thomas challenge (14:5)? Do you think Jesus answered the way Thomas expected? Why or why not?

♦ **6.** Thomas is assuming that unless he knows *where* Jesus is going he cannot know *how* to get there, but Jesus has told him he already knows the way. What did Jesus mean when he said that (14:4)?

♦ **7.** What does Jesus mean when he says, "I am the way" in 14:6?

To whom, what, or where is he the way?

♦ **8.** Do you think Philip has figured out what Jesus means about being the way (14:8)? Explain.

♦ **9.** Jesus says that anyone who has seen him has seen the Father (14:9). Why does he say that we see the Father by looking at him (Jesus)? What qualifies him to show us the Father?

♦ **10.** Why can't we come to the Father except through Jesus?

♦ **11.** When you consider Jesus as "the way," do you think of him mostly as a way to get to heaven and escape hell, or do you think of him as the way to know the Father and have a relationship with him? What's the difference?

12. Many people feel that Jesus is merely one of many good people who have pointed the way to God. What is the difference between *pointing* the way and *being* the way?

13. Have you ever asked Jesus to be your way to the Father? If so, tell something about your faith journey so far. If not, try to identify what it is that hinders you from seeing Jesus as your way. Is it fear? Unbelief? Lack of information? The studies that follow will help you know this Jesus who claims to be the way to God.

"I AM THE GATE"

John 10:1-10; Matthew 7:13-14

As I entered the maximum security prison in Joliet, Illinois, the huge steel gate clanged shut behind me. I felt a quick knot form in my stomach and shuddered while waiting for the next door (or gate) to open. What if a terrible mistake happened and I was trapped forever?

Although I was only there to help present a worship service, that momentary terror caused me to think how terrible it must be for people who enter knowing there will never be a way out. Those gates totally control who is on the inside or outside of that prison. Until they are opened, no individual can be admitted or released.

"I am the gate," Jesus said. What did he mean by likening himself to a gate or a door? Today's study will help us find out.

1. Describe a time when an imposing gate made you feel left out and unwanted, or conversely, safe and included.

Read John 10:1-10.

2. A sheep pen is a four-walled structure where sheep are brought at night. What is the purpose of the walls in this structure?

3. What is the purpose of the gate in the sheep pen?

4. Why don't thieves and robbers use the gate?

Read Matthew 7:13-14 and re-read John 10:9-10.

♦ **5.** These verses imply that the gate is a specific place where we enter into something. What are we entering?

♦ **6.** From what are we being saved when we enter the gate (John 10:9-10)?

7. Why is Jesus the *narrow* gate?

♦ **8.** Why do people prefer the wide gate, even if it leads to destruction?

♦ **9.** Although we most often think of Jesus as being the gate to "eternal life"—by which we mean life after we die, the picture in John 10 offers more than that. Why do the sheep need to go in and out of the gate (John 10:9)?

What does this picture mean to us?

♦ **10.** What kind of life is Jesus talking about in John 10:10?

11. In what way do you need Jesus to be your gate?

"I AM THE GOOD SHEPHERD"

John 10:1-33

What a warm and loving relationship exists between a shepherd and his sheep. He knows them by name, and they know him by his voice. In spite of this, sheep are prone to go off on their own, to wander away, and get lost. Without the shepherd to lead them, sheep cannot find their own way to pasture, or even back home. Once separated from the shepherd, they are also in great danger, for they have no natural defenses (such as outstanding speed or piercing antlers) against other predators.

In this study, we see the heart of a true shepherd who understands how totally vulnerable his sheep are without his care. There is never a hint of frustration in the shepherd that these sheep are so dependent on him. It is only the tenderness of his love that shines through.

1. Describe a time when you felt lost and afraid, perhaps even as a child, and someone came and rescued you.

Read John 10:1-33.

2. List the various characters in this chapter, along with their characteristics. Who or what might these characters represent?

3. How is Jesus the good shepherd (verses 11-17, 25-30)? How do his feelings for the sheep compare to those of the hired hand or the robber?

♦ **4.** What are characteristics of sheep?

5. How are we like sheep?

6. Although a shepherd speaks to his sheep, it is unlikely they can fully understand where he is taking them each day. Why are they so willing to follow him when they don't know exactly where they are going or how they will get there?

7. Why does the shepherd go in front of the sheep (verse 4)?

◆ **8.** How do sheep learn to distinguish the shepherd's voice from all others (verses 4-5)?

9. How does Jesus compare the relationship of the sheep to himself with his own relationship to the Father (verses 14-17)?

10. What are some of the dangers that sheep face (verses 11-13)? How does the shepherd protect them?

11. What are some dangers that we face? How does Jesus as our shepherd protect us?

♦ **12.** Who are the "other sheep" Jesus talks about (verse 16)? What is his desire for them?

13. In today's world of conflicting messages, it is comforting to know that Jesus promises we will be able to distinguish his voice from all others. How does he speak to us? How have you learned to hear his voice?

"I AM THE TRUTH"

John 14:6, 15-31; 16:5-15

When Jesus was on trial, he said he had come to the world to testify to the truth. Then Pontius Pilate asked him the age-old question, "What is truth?"

For many, it is very difficult to believe that there is any definite answer to Pilate's question. In his book, *Situation Ethics,* Joseph Fletcher claimed that all truth was relative to the situation in which it was applied. He believed there was no such thing as absolute, universal truth.

In our first study, we looked at Jesus' claim to be the only way to the Father (John 14:6). In this study we look at the second claim Jesus made in that same verse. "I am the truth." Is there such a thing as truth? How can a person claim to *be* truth rather than *teach* it? Why do we have to know Jesus as the truth to come to the Father?

1. Is there such a thing as absolute, ultimate, non-negotiable truth? If you say yes, how do you define truth? If you say no, why?

How can we discover truth?

Read John 14:6, 15-31.

2. As you read this, how would you describe Jesus' relationship to the Father?

3. Why can Jesus reveal the truth of who the Father is to us?

♦ **4.** All through this passage, Jesus keeps saying that those who love him will keep his commandments. Does his being the truth give him the right to expect obedience? Why or why not?

5. Our culture assumes there are different compartments for "truth"—e.g., scientific, spiritual, pragmatic, physical. Are these distinctions valid? Is there any such thing as "secular truth"?

Read John 16:5-15.

♦ **6.** Who is this Spirit of truth Jesus says will come? When did (or does) he come?

7. Why is it better for the Spirit of truth to be here than for Jesus to have stayed on earth?

8. What truth(s) is the Spirit of truth going to reveal to the world (verses 8-11)?

9. What else is the Spirit going to do (verses 12-15)?

♦ **10.** Why do we have to know Jesus as the truth in order to come to the Father?

11. What is your response to the fact that Jesus is the truth?

"I AM THE LIGHT"
Part 1

John 8:1-30

One day, while living overseas, I impulsively invited the American ambassador to our home for dinner. When he graciously accepted, I immediately regretted my rash proposal. We lived at the end of a poorly maintained road with enough bumps to make anyone carsick. The coat of paint on our house was covered with mildew from the tropical dampness. My furniture was well worn. I didn't even have a set of matching silverware because thieves had stolen half of each set the year before. Compared to the parties hosted at the ambassador's splendid residence, my offerings seemed meager indeed.

Imagine my joy when one of our frequent power outages happened fifteen minutes before the ambassador's arrival! I laughed as I lit our ever-ready candles. Now he could barely see his food, let alone the surroundings. I hoped the lights would stay off until he left. Thankfully, they did. He never saw anything but a lovely candlelight dinner!

Sometimes we prefer to live in spiritual darkness—not wanting God, others, or ourselves to see the shabbiness of sin deep within us. In this study Christ reveals himself as the light who shines in even those hidden spaces.

1. Can you recall trying to use darkness to hide something? If so, what was it and why?

Take a few minutes to think about light. What are its qualities? What does it *do?*

Read John 8:1-30.

◆ **2.** Who are the Pharisees? Why are they bringing this woman to Jesus?

3. In verses 5-6, what is the trap the Pharisees want to set for Jesus? Why?

♦ **4.** Jesus immediately follows this incident with his statement that he is the light of the world (verse 12). What is the darkness he refers to in this verse? What is this light of life?

5. What has this light just revealed about the Pharisees (verses 3-9)? What does it continue to reveal (verses 23-24)?

6. How do you think the Pharisees felt after Jesus spoke to them? Can you think of a time when you felt a similar way?

♦ **7.** Verse 27 states that the Pharisees didn't understand what Jesus was saying. Why do you think they were unable to understand?

Name some things that prevent us from seeing clearly or understanding situations.

8. What has Jesus' light revealed to the woman in verses 10-11? How did this show her the Father?

9. How do you think the woman felt after Christ spoke to her? In what way, if any, can you relate to her feelings?

10. Do you think Jesus' words to the Pharisees in verse 7 mean we are never to judge sin in others? Explain your answer.

11. Can you think of a time when the light of Jesus revealed something about who you are that you never knew before?

12. List promises or warnings in these verses that can serve as light in your life.

"I AM THE LIGHT"
Part 2

John 9

When we lived in Africa, our frequent electrical power outages were due to a low supply of fuel in the country. Our home, at the end of a long road, was the last one supplied by the electrical line. Without power, the darkness was intense because no street lights or neon signs lit the night. In that darkness, it was impossible to do any work. Even reading was a major chore by candlelight. But we always knew a split second before our lights came back on that electricity was on its way—we could hear the cheers of our neighbors as current surged down the line and their own lights returned to full brilliance.

We had one neighbor, however, who never cheered. He never knew if the lights were off or on, because he was blind. Without light, even good eyes can't see, but no amount of light can change the darkness for those without healthy eyes.

In this study we see Jesus bringing the joy of both physical and spiritual light to one who had lived in darkness all his life.

1. What do you think it would be like to be physically blind?

Read John 9.

♦ **2.** A world view is an underlying assumption about the reasons for what we see happening in our world. What is the disciples' world view as reflected in their question to Jesus (verse 2)?

♦ **3.** How might our western world view be reflected in a similar question about a blind person today?

4. How might Jesus' answer to our question be the same or different from the one he gave the disciples in verses 3-5?

5. Once again, Jesus teaches spiritual lessons by using ordinary circumstances to illustrate his points. Why does he choose this moment in verse 5 to reiterate that he is the light of the world?

♦ **6.** What is Jesus' part in the blind man's healing (verses 6-7)? What is the man's part? Whose part actually healed him?

7. How do the neighbors and others who have known this person as a blind man react (verses 8-12)? Why?

8. Why are the Pharisees investigating this miracle so carefully (verses 13-34)? What is upsetting them?

9. How do the parents react to the situation (verses 18-23)? Can you relate to their response? If so, how?

10. Throughout all the turmoil of the various reactions (verses 8-34), how does the formerly blind man respond? Why is he able to react this way?

11. Suddenly, there is a new response from the blind man (verses 35-38). What has changed for him?

♦ **12.** Jesus completes the metaphor of blindness and light in verses 39-41. What kind of blindness is he talking about here? How is he the light in that kind of darkness?

13. Has there been a time in your life when God changed your spiritual blindness to sight in such a specific, healing way that you did not need to defend or explain it—you simply *knew* it as this man did? Is there some place of confusion, pain, bitterness, or sin in your life where you know you still need new spiritual eyes to see his light? Would you ask him now?

"I AM THE RESURRECTION"
Part 1

John 11:1-44; Romans 6:1-14

In her book, *Running on Empty,* Jill Briscoe reflects on the two heart cries we long to direct toward God. The first is, "God, are you there?" The second, and, as Jill says, the far harder question is, "If you're there, do you care?"

Perhaps one of life's darkest moments is when we have cried out to God and we know he *could* change our painful situation, but he doesn't. The silence is deafening as we wonder why there seems to be no answer.

As we examine the backdrop of Jesus' triumphal statement, "I am the resurrection and the life," we see that this was one of those dark moments for Mary and Martha. But we will also discover how tenderly Jesus dealt with them in their sorrow.

1. Have you ever asked someone for something and been totally ignored? How did you feel?

Read John 11:1-6.

2. What was Jesus' relationship to Mary, Martha, and Lazarus? Given their relationship, what kind of response would Mary and Martha most likely have expected from Jesus at this time?

Read John 11:7-37.

3. From these verses, how would you describe Martha? (Consider her reactions: feelings, faith, the whole personality.)

How would you describe Mary?

4. Mary and Martha use the same words when they first meet Jesus. Based on what they said and did after their initial statements to Jesus, do you think there is a difference in how they said these words? If so, in what way? If not, how are they the same?

♦ **5.** How does Jesus deal differently with their specific personalities? Do you identify most with Mary or with Martha in how they reacted to suffering?

6. Jesus declares that he *is* the resurrection and the life (verse 25). What kind of death is being discussed in this verse? What kinds of death are there besides physical death?

Read Romans 6:1-14.

♦ **7.** If one wants to walk in a resurrected life, what kind of death will have to happen first?

8. In what kind of life will a person never die?

Read John 11:38-44.

9. How do you think Mary and Martha felt when Lazarus was raised? Why was this miracle so important that Jesus let them endure all the pain beforehand?

10. Why did Jesus weep when he knew everything was going to be all right (verse 35)?

Do you believe Jesus has ever wept with you?

11. Have you ever tried to explain to God, as Martha did (verse 39), why something he seems to be asking you to do is not a very good idea? Tell your story.

12. In Galatians 2:20 Paul says, "I have been crucified with Christ and I no longer live, but Christ lives in me. The life I live in the body, I live by faith in the Son of God, who loved me and gave himself for me." Have you, or are you willing to submit to letting your "old self," or sinful nature, be crucified with Christ that you too might live a new life by faith in Jesus Christ?

"I AM THE RESURRECTION"
Part 2

1 Corinthians 15

Often we think of resurrection only as an event to be celebrated on Easter—something that happened to Jesus a long time ago. When Jesus says, "I am the resurrection," he states it as an eternal, on-going reality as well as a one-time, historical occurrence.

In our last study, we saw resurrection not only as something that happens after physical death, but also as the beginning of our new spiritual life.

The second part of our study on resurrection focuses on the reality that Jesus is the forerunner for our own bodily resurrection.

1. When you were a child, what were your images or ideas of life after death? Where did you learn them?

Read 1 Corinthians 15:1-11.

> **2.** Paul says that Jesus' death and resurrection are "of first importance" (verse 3). Why are they so important?

♦ **3.** Why would Paul bother to list specific people who saw Jesus after his resurrection (verses 5-8)?

♦ **4.** When do you think Paul saw Jesus (verse 8)?

Read 1 Corinthians 15:12-19.

> **5.** Among the Jews, the Sadducees had always proclaimed that there was no life after death for anyone. Now Paul is concerned that someone is teaching the same heresy to these Gentile Christians. Why does Paul consider it such an important issue to clarify?

6. Why should Christians be "pitied more than all men" if our hope in Jesus is for this life alone (verse 19)?

Read 1 Corinthians 15:20-58.

◆ **7.** What is Jesus' role in our own resurrection? What does it mean that "as in Adam all die, so in Christ all will be made alive" (verses 20-22, 45-55)?

8. Why can't flesh and blood inherit the kingdom of God nor the "perishable inherit the imperishable" (verse 50)?

9. Without God's direct revelation, we could not know anything about life after death. Looking at Jesus as the prototype of resurrection (verses 35-54), what specific facts do you learn about your future life?

♦ **10.** How do these truths about our resurrection compare with the doctrine of reincarnation (the belief that the same soul comes back to life here on earth over and over)?

11. Some people accuse Christians of having an escapist mentality because of their belief in eternal life. Paul seems to have the opposite view. How does Paul tie the hope of resurrection to our life here and now (verse 58)?

12. Do you ever feel your life has no real purpose or significance—that you do indeed labor in vain? How can the hope of resurrection change the way you view your present life?

"I AM THE LIFE"

John 14:6; 17:1-3; 3:1-18

After my first patient died when I was a young student nurse, I stared at the body in wonder at the mystery of life. Every tangible thing I had cared for was there, but the person was gone. *Where did she go? I wondered. What is life anyway? Why did her body function before and now it is so cold and silent? Is this life the only one? What makes this life worth living if this is how you end up? Is there another life? If so, what is it? Where is it?*

These were hard questions for a nineteen-year-old, but questions that needed to be answered. Jesus says he is the life, but he must mean something different than mere physical life. He is speaking to people who have already been born physically, telling them that without him as the life, they cannot see the Father. What *is* this life Jesus says he is? Why is it so important?

1. How does our culture define a life that is worth living?

Read John 14:6.

    2. What kind of life do you think Jesus is talking about here?

Read John 17:1-3.

◆ **3.** According to Jesus, what is eternal life? How is that different from the way we usually think of it?

    4. What does it mean to "know" the Father and Jesus?

Read John 3:1-18.

5. Jesus says without being "born again," a person cannot see the kingdom of God. What does it mean to be "born again" (verses 3, 5-8)? What is the first birth?

♦ 6. A kingdom is, by definition, a place where a king or queen has the power and authority to rule. Thus, the kingdom of God is where God rules. How is this different from this earth's kingdom?

♦ 7. Jesus says we can neither *see* nor *enter* the kingdom of God without this new birth. Why?

♦ 8. How is Jesus this new life (verses 14-17)? What does it mean to "believe in Jesus"? How is this different from believing in God?

9. Why are we condemned if we do not believe in Jesus (verse 18)? Is it possible to be neutral about Jesus? Explain your answer.

10. Do you think Nicodemus "believed in Jesus"? Why or why not?

11. Do you know, for sure, that you have had the spiritual birth Jesus talked about? Take this time to pray with one another that each of you can see Jesus' light, believe in him as the way, truth, and life, and be part of that kingdom of God where the Father rules over all.

"I AM THE VINE"

John 15:1-17

Early each spring, my husband carefully plants tomato seeds in small biodegradable pots. He nurtures the seedlings with warmth and water inside our garage until the day he can transplant them to his garden. After that, he simply checks their growth daily, pinches off a few dead leaves, gives a little extra water if it hasn't rained—and waits. There is no way to rush the fruit that will come, but by the end of summer, this simple process results in my kitchen counter overflowing with luscious red tomatoes that supply not only our needs but are passed to many friends and neighbors as well.

Today we look at one of the great paradoxes of God's ways with us: that we accomplish far more by resting in him than by actively pursuing endless activities—even the activities we do in his name. Understanding this truth can set us free for the abundant, joyful life Jesus came to give us.

1. Do you like to raise plants or make a garden? If so, what do you find gratifying about it? If not, why not?

Read John 15:1-17.

2. In the natural world, what does the vine do so that the plant can bear fruit?

3. What does the branch do in the same process?

4. How does the gardener or vinedresser help the plant to be more productive?

5. Why does Jesus say he is the vine (verse 1)?

6. Why does Jesus say we are the branches (verse 5)?

♦ **7.** What is the fruit we will bear (verses 2-5)?

8. What does it mean to remain (or to abide) in Jesus and he in us?

9. How do we do that (verses 5-17)?

♦ **10.** Why is pruning essential for increased fruitbearing (verse 2)? How does God prune us?

11. If you feel God's pruning in your life, why should that encourage you?

12. What is Jesus' basic command to the disciples (verse 12)? How does obeying Jesus' commandments result in a joyful, fruitful life (verses 9-17)?

13. What comfort does verse 16 give you as you face the circumstances of your own life?

"I AM THE BREAD"

John 6:22-51

Do you ever feel spiritually starved? Jesus says he is the bread of life, the only one who can satisfy your hunger for fullness of life.

Often we bypass God and look for other ways to fill that empty hole within. It seems impossible that he is truly enough to meet life's deepest longings. We search for satisfaction in our mates, children, jobs, ministry, or friends. Some of us try drugs or sex; others feverishly pursue riches or pleasure. We spend countless hours doing more, acquiring more, running more, playing more, but the emptiness is never filled. Soon we are so exhausted with all this effort that there is neither time nor energy left to enjoy the true bread of life.

As you study today, come with the hope that there *is* a way to be truly satisfied. Ask God to show you what it means not only to taste the living bread, but to have your whole life sustained by it.

1. What does it feel like to be hungry? What kinds of hunger do you see in yourself and the people you know?

Read John 6:22-51.

2. On the day before this event, Jesus miraculously fed 5,000 people with five loaves and two fish. How does this miracle serve as a backdrop to Christ's statement, "I am the bread of life" (verses 35, 41, 48)?

♦ **3.** What is bread? How is it made?

Why do we need bread? What is its function?

4. Jesus calls himself "the bread." Why might he have chosen to use this particular metaphor with these people?

5. What was manna, and where did it come from? What did it demonstrate to the Israelites about God? (See Exodus 16:4-5, 31-35.)

♦ **6.** Compare and contrast the manna from the Old Testament with Jesus (verses 25-35, 48-51). How did that manna portray Christ who was to come?

♦ **7.** How did the Jews react to Christ's claim that he was the bread of life (look especially at verses 41-42, 52)? Why?

8. To become useful, bread must be eaten. How do you "eat Christ" and receive this life (verses 35, 47-51)?

9. What is the difference between working for physical bread and working for spiritual bread (verses 26-29)?

10. What hunger does Christ satisfy (verse 35)? What life does he sustain (verses 51, 54, 57-58)?

11. What are some ways you have tried to satisfy your own hunger for love, meaning, purpose, or significance?

12. What difference does it make in your life today that Christ is the bread of life? Have you tasted of him personally yet?

"I AM THE ALPHA AND OMEGA"

Revelation 1; John 1:1-5, 10-14

As my mother and I sat together sewing dresses for my sister's upcoming wedding, Mom reflected on her own marriage.

"You know, when I married your dad, I believed I really loved him. Now, twenty-five years later, I love him so much more. Sometimes I wonder, *How did I ever dare marry him with such a little bit of love compared to what I have now?* It's kind of scary to think about!"

The beauty of good relationships is the way they continue to grow and grow. We love someone and think we know all there is to know about him or her, when suddenly we are surprised by a new tenderness, a new depth of integrity we never saw before.

John thought he knew Jesus. After all, they had been together almost daily for three years. He was the disciple "whom Jesus loved." While dying on the cross, Jesus entrusted the care of his own mother to John. During Jesus' time on earth, no one knew him better than John did.

Sometime after Jesus ascended into heaven, John saw Jesus in a brand-new way. In this study we will look at this final revelation of

Jesus to John—and what it means when Jesus says, "I am the Alpha and Omega."

1. How does language make humans different from all other species? What would our communication with each other be like without language?

Read Revelation 1.

2. What is the picture we see here of Jesus as the Alpha and Omega (verses 8, 12-16)? How does this vision of Jesus compare with the way we have seen him in the Gospels?

Note: Alpha and omega are the first and last letters of the Greek alphabet.

3. By all accounts, this John is the same writer as the one who wrote the Gospel of John. How does he identify himself in verse 9?

4. John had often seen Jesus before as they walked and talked together. Why do you think he fell down as one who was dead this time (verse 17)?

Read John 1:1-5, 10-14.

5. Why do you think God chose to use terms like *Word* and *Alpha and Omega* when describing Jesus?

♦ **6.** Jesus came as the living Word of God. What did Jesus reveal about God that we couldn't understand any other way?

♦ **7.** Alpha and Omega are the first and last letters in the Greek alphabet, like A and Z are in ours. In verses 1-3 and 10, what do we learn of Jesus as the Alpha?

♦ **8.** In verse 14, John tells of seeing Jesus' glory while he lived among them on earth. When do you think it might have been? Was it the same glory John saw again in Revelation 1?

9. Who is this Jesus, the Alpha and Omega? List what you find about him in Revelation 1:4-8, 17-18.

10. How many of the other "I ams" we have studied do you see reflected here?

11. What does it mean to you that Jesus is the one "who is, and who was, and who is to come, the Almighty" (Revelation 1:8)?

LEADER'S NOTES

■ **Study 1/"I Am the Way"**

Question 6. Here Jesus is affirming the faith the disciples already have. They remain confused about many things, but somehow they still trust him enough to continue to go with him. That is the essence of faith—to trust Jesus because of who he is—the Son of God, the Messiah, the Savior, the Way, Faithful, True, and so on—not *simply* trusting in what he did.

Question 7. It is important to note that Jesus is not merely going to a place such as heaven. He is also going to a person, the Father. The whole focus on Jesus' ministry was to show us and lead us to the Father. That needs to be stressed at the beginning of this series.

Question 8. Philip doesn't understand exactly what Jesus means either, but he does switch from asking about getting to a place to asking to see a person. The truth of what Jesus is saying is beginning to emerge.

Question 9. Jesus says over and over that when we see him we have seen the Father, for they are completely one in thought, purpose, and desire. (John 8:19; 10:30; and 12:45 are some references that state this truth.) Jesus is also the only one qualified to show us the Father because he is the only one who has actually seen him. Matthew 11:27 says, "No one knows the Son except the Father, and no one knows the Father except the Son and those to whom the Son chooses to reveal him."

Question 10. We have absolutely no way in our own reasoning to understand who God is without God revealing it to us. 1 Timothy 2:5-6 says there is only "one mediator between God and men, the man Christ Jesus, who gave himself as a ransom for all men." Since sin entered the world (Genesis 3), the judgment for sin has been death. When Christ came, he, who had never sinned, died to pay the price for our sins (Galatians 3:13; Hebrews 2:9; 1 John 3:5). We have no other basis on which to come to the Father except by accepting the substitution of Jesus' death for our own.

Question 11. If Jesus is *only* the way to heaven, then we see our relationship with God primarily as something for the future rather than something to be enjoyed now.

■ Study 2/"I Am the Gate"

Question 5. Jesus tells us in other Scripture that we enter eternal life through him (John 5:24; 6:40; 20:31). He also says we enter the kingdom of God (Mark 10:15). In Hebrews, we see that through Jesus we can enter into the very presence of God (Hebrews 10:19-22).

Question 6. Satan is the one who steals, kills, and destroys. One of the things Jesus came to do was to save us from this destruction in our present lives as well as in the life to come.

Question 8. Humankind's original sin had to do with the lure of having power and knowledge apart from God. Ever since then, people have preferred to construct their own "god" the way they see fit rather than submit to who God really is.

Question 9. Sheep need to go outside the sheepfold to find food and water, to exercise, and to get fresh air. But they also need to rest in a protected place, safe from predators who would attack and destroy them.

Likewise, Christ's sheep need to move out into the world, to work, to live, and to take Christ to others. But they also need a place for protection and rest for themselves. This is where Christ is the gate that stands as protection against the onslaught of Satan's destructive tactics. Jesus stands as the strong gate between us and the worries, troubles, and cares that disturb us, so we can find a place of inner quiet to rest and be refreshed with God.

Question 10. Having life "to the full" is not necessarily the world's idea of fullness. It is not in the abundance of things a person possesses (Luke 12:15-25), but in being a servant (Mark 10:42-45). Jesus promises that when we have laid down our lives to find them in him, there will be blessings far greater than we can imagine (Luke 18:29-30).

◼ Study 3/"I Am the Good Shepherd"

Question 4. Sheep have no natural protection or inherent sense of danger; they are prone to wander from the flock and get lost; they cannot find their own way home; they have no idea where the best pasture is. Encourage group members to think of more characteristics.

Question 8. Sheep learn to recognize the shepherd through day-by-day exposure. The shepherd speaks to them as he comes to the gate, he calls them and leads them out. The more they are with him, the more familiar his voice becomes.

Question 12. John 10:16 refers to all who do not yet know Jesus, whom he will be calling to himself. In a broader picture, however, it also refers to the fact that salvation will soon be opened to the Gentiles. The old covenant was made between God and Abraham for his descendants. Now the spiritual promises are being extended to all who will believe and enter into the promises through faith and spiritual birth, not merely physical birth.

■ Study 4/"I Am the Truth"

Question 4. Many people would like to have Jesus be their way to get to heaven and escape hell, but they do not want to submit to Jesus as the truth for how life is to be lived in God's kingdom here on earth.

Question 6. The Spirit of truth is the Holy Spirit of God who came to fill the disciples with his power at Pentecost (Acts 2:1-4). It is that same Spirit who comes to us to give us spiritual birth as we believe in Jesus (John 3:5-8, 16).

Question 10. Through our own wisdom, we can only guess at truth. A god created by our reasoning alone is necessarily subject to the limitations of our finite perspective. This is why we can only know the truth of who God is through what *God* reveals to us about himself, and he has chosen to reveal himself through Jesus Christ.

■ Study 5/"I Am the Light," Part 1

Question 2. The Pharisees were the religious rulers of the Jews. The law God gave to Moses stated that if a man committed adultery with another man's wife, both the adulterer and adulteress must be put to death (Leviticus 20:10). It is interesting that there is no mention of the fate of the male partner in this situation.

Question 4. Jesus has rescued us from the dominion of darkness and brought us into the kingdom of light (Colossians 1:12-14). The darkness of Satan's deception is exposed when Jesus comes as the light.

Question 7. John 8:23 helps us understand this question. The Pharisees were only seeing with human eyes; they were unable to perceive heavenly truths. Another passage of Scripture that lends insight to the religious establishment's inability to recognize Jesus is found in 2 Corinthians 3:13-16. These verses tell us that *when a person turns his or her heart* to God, understanding of God's truth is given. Thus, it was not impossible for religious leaders to discover Jesus as God's Son.

■ **Study 6/"I Am the Light," Part 2**

Question 2. The disciples assumed that all misfortunes such as blindness were a punishment for specific sin.

Question 3. In our day, the first question might be, "Who can we sue for malpractice?" Our Western world view believes everything has a logical, scientific reason for its occurrence. It presumes people can control the outcome of almost everything once they understand the rules of how a tornado, virus, bacteria, atom, or DNA works. Any bad outcome means someone slipped up somewhere and they should have to pay. There is little or no place for simple misfortune—or God's purposes, which are often not comprehensible to us.

Question 6. In every miracle performed by Jesus—including our salvation—all the power is from him. Yet, in one of the paradoxes of faith, when Jesus wants to do something for a person, he asks for a response from that man or woman. His or her response becomes an act of true faith. It was in going to wash the mud off his eyes that the blind man showed he truly believed in who Jesus was, the one who had the power to heal him.

Question 12. 2 Corinthians 4:4 says that the god of this age, or Satan, "has blinded the minds of unbelievers, so that they cannot see the light of the . . . glory of Christ, who is the image of God." Jesus came to give spiritual sight to all of us who are spiritually blind. When our spiritual sight is restored, the light with which we see is Jesus.

■ Study 7/"I Am the Resurrection," Part 1

Question 5. Jesus knows the differences of our personalities and how we need to deal with things. With Martha, he discusses the issue; with Mary, he simply weeps with her in her pain. There are no words necessary at this point.

Question 7. Romans 6:1-14 tells us that our sin nature, or "old self" must be crucified with Christ if we are to walk with him in the new life. We must be "united with him . . . in his death" to be "united with him in his resurrection" (Romans 6:5).

■ Study 8/"I Am the Resurrection," Part 2

Question 3. This was to validate that Jesus had a *bodily* resurrection rather than merely some spiritualized or symbolic version. If his readers wanted proof, these were the people with whom they could check.

Question 4. No one knows if Paul actually saw Jesus during his days on earth, but Acts 9:1-6 tells of how Paul did see Jesus on the way to Damascus when he was converted.

Question 7. Without Jesus paying the price for the sin that came on all humankind through Adam, there would be no resurrection. It is only by his power and authority that we can be resurrected. Jesus has also gone before to show us how we will go.

Question 10. Hebrews 9:27-28 says, "Just as man is destined to die once, and after that to face judgment, so Christ was sacrificed once to take away the sins of many." Life is not in a repeating cycle. Each resurrection body has one earthly body that was planted as its "seed."

■ Study 9/"I Am the Life"

Question 3. "Eternal life" is usually equated as something for later, after we die on earth. Jesus defines it clearly as being a relationship with his Father. It is one that begins with new birth and never, ever ends.

Question 6. The kingdom of God is where his rule and righteousness reign. It is opposite in every way to the kingdom of this world. In God's kingdom, we are to lose our lives in order to find them. In the earthly kingdom, we are told to grab all the gusto we can get because we are only going around life once. Think of other contrasts between the two kingdoms.

Question 7. Just as we need physical birth to enter the physical world, so we need spiritual birth to enter the spiritual world, or kingdom (John 3:5).

Question 8. Jesus makes new life possible through his death for us on the cross. We receive it by believing *in* Jesus, not merely believing facts *about* Jesus. John 8:24 says, "If you do not believe *that I am the one I claim to be, you will indeed die in your sins*"; 1 John 5:1

says, "Everyone who believes *that Jesus is the Christ* is born of God" (emphases mine). Why is this so important? Because many are willing to believe in some vague notion about God, but far fewer are willing to believe that Jesus is who he said he is.

■ Study 10/"I Am the Vine"

Question 7. Often people define the *fruit* as how many people you lead to the Lord. Biblical fruit, however, is defined in Galatians 5:22-23 as "the fruit of the Spirit"—love, joy, peace, patience, kindness, goodness, faithfulness, gentleness, and self-control.

Question 10. If there are too many extra leaves and branches on a plant, all the nutrients from the vine are dissipated to them rather than into making fruit. Too much pruning, however, can kill a plant. A gardener must know how much to cut in order to keep the plant thriving and healthy, and what to leave so that the plant is not destroyed.

One way God prunes us is through circumstances which may force us to trust him more. Another way is through his Word, exposing attitudes or sin that need to be dealt with. Can you think of more ways?

■ Study 11/"I Am the Bread"

Question 3. Bread is a staple in most diets, the commonest form of food, yet it comes in different styles in various cultures. It is relatively cheap and thus available even to poor people. While bread is readily available once it has been prepared, the preparation of bread is an arduous procedure. First the grain of wheat must be broken and ground. Then the dough must be mixed and set aside until it rises. In cultures where one cannot easily buy bread at a local supermarket, one must plan well ahead to make sure it is made.

Question 6. Exodus 16:1-36 is the story of God's provision of manna for the Israelites while they were wandering in the wilderness for forty years. The manna was their daily sustenance. If they missed it for a day or two, they would be hungry. If they refused it altogether, they would die. It was bread provided directly from heaven. While manna sustained physical life, Jesus says that the Father is giving true bread that will sustain spiritual life.

Question 7. Since the whole crowd was presumably Jewish, "the Jews" in these verses likely refers to the religious leaders. Because they had studied the Old Testament, these leaders were well aware that Jesus was claiming to be the Messiah when he compared himself to manna as he claimed to be the "bread of heaven." In John 5:18, the Jews had already tried to kill him because "he was even calling God his own Father, making himself equal with God." To them, this was blasphemy, one of the worst sins possible.

Apparently their opinions were divided. Some believed that Jesus could be no other than the Messiah because of the miracles he did. Others could only see that he was an ordinary man like themselves, with a family they could name. They wondered how a mere man—a "local"—could be the promised Messiah.

■ Study 12/"I Am the Alpha and Omega"

Question 6. Jesus became God who we could see, whose character we could easily observe, and whose love we could tangibly experience as human to human—yet his love went far beyond normal human love. Jesus' willingness to come to earth and die on a cross proved the greatest love humankind has ever known. We can believe that love because we have seen it lived out before us.

Question 7. Before Jesus ever became a man, he was with the Father at Creation. Nothing was created without him. He has been with the

Father through all eternity, from the beginning to the end of our human history. No wonder he alone can show us the Father!

Question 8. This probably reflects the time John was on the Mount of Olives when Jesus was transfigured (Matthew 17:1-9). This was John's initial vision of the glory of Jesus.

WHAT SHOULD WE STUDY NEXT?

To help your group answer that question, we've listed the Fisherman Guides by category so you can choose your next study.

TOPICAL STUDIES

Angels, Wright

Becoming Women of Purpose, Barton

Building Your House on the Lord, Brestin

The Creative Heart of God, Goring

Discipleship, Reapsome

Doing Justice, Showing Mercy, Wright

Encouraging Others, Johnson

The End Times, Rusten

Examining the Claims of Jesus, Brestin

Friendship, Brestin

The Fruit of the Spirit, Briscoe

Great Doctrines of the Bible, Board

Great Passages of the Bible, Plueddemann

Great Prayers of the Bible, Plueddemann

Growing Through Life's Challenges, Reapsome

Guidance & God's Will, Stark

Heart Renewal, Goring

Higher Ground, Brestin

Images of Redemption, Van Reken

Integrity, Engstrom & Larson

Lifestyle Priorities, White

Marriage, Stevens

Miracles, Castleman

One Body, One Spirit, Larsen

The Parables of Jesus, Hunt

Prayer, Jones

The Prophets, Wright

Proverbs & Parables, Brestin

Satisfying Work, Stevens & Schoberg

Senior Saints, Reapsome

Sermon on the Mount, Hunt

Spiritual Gifts, Dockrey

A Spiritual Legacy, Christensen

Spiritual Warfare, Moreau

The Ten Commandments, Briscoe

Ultimate Hope for Changing Times, Larsen

Who Is God? Seemuth

Who Is Jesus? Van Reken

Who Is the Holy Spirit? Knuckles & Van Reken

Wisdom for Today's Woman: Insights from Esther, Smith

Witnesses to All the World, Plueddemann

Women at Midlife, Miley

Worship, Sibley

BIBLE BOOK STUDIES

Genesis, Fromer & Keyes
Exodus, Larsen
Job, Klug
Psalms, Klug
Proverbs: Wisdom That Works,
  Wright
Jeremiah, Reapsome
Jonah, Habakkuk, & Malachi,
  Fromer & Keyes
Matthew, Sibley
Mark, Christensen
Luke, Keyes
John: Living Word, Kuniholm
Acts 1-12, Christensen
Paul (Acts 13-28), Christiansen
Romans: The Christian
  Story, Reapsome
1 Corinthians, Hummel

Strengthened to Serve
  (2 Corinthians),
  Plueddemann
Galatians, Titus & Philemon,
  Kuniholm
Ephesians, Baylis
Philippians, Klug
Colossians, Shaw
Letters to the Thessalonians,
  Fromer & Keyes
Letters to Timothy, Fromer &
  Keyes
Hebrews, Hunt
James, Christensen
1 & 2 Peter, Jude, Brestin
How Should a Christian Live?
  (1, 2 & 3 John), Brestin
Revelation, Hunt

BIBLE CHARACTER STUDIES

David: Man after God's Own
  Heart, Castleman
Elijah, Castleman
Great People of the Bible,
  Plueddemann
King David: Trusting God for
  a Lifetime, Castleman
Men Like Us, Heidebrecht &
  Scheuermann

Moses, Asimakoupoulos
Paul (Acts 13-28), Christensen
Women Like Us, Barton
Women Who Achieved for
  God, Christensen
Women Who Believed God,
  Christensen